About the Author

Magenta Pixie is a channel for the higher dimensional, divine intelligence known as 'The White Winged Collective Consciousness of Nine'. The transmissions she receives from 'The Nine' have reached thousands of people worldwide via the extensive video collection on her YouTube channel. She has worked with people from all over the world as an intuitive consultant and ascension/consciousness coach. Magenta lives in the New Forest, UK

Visit Magenta Pixie online at www.magentapixie.com

Also by Magenta Pixie

~ Books ~

Masters of the Matrix:
Becoming the Architect of Your Reality and
Activating the Original Human Template

Divine Architecture and the Starseed Template:
Matrix Memory Triggers for Ascension

The Infinite Helix and the Emerald Flame:
Sacred Mysteries of Stargate Ascension

~ MP3 Guided Meditation Collections ~

Gateways Within

Euphoric Voyage

Sacred Quest

Elemental Dream

Cover design by Daniel Saunders

Author photograph by Oliver McGuire of Visual Logistics

Print Edition 1, 2019

ISBN: 9781092164016

White Spirit Publishing
www.magentapixie.com
enquiries: magenta.pixie@mail.com

The Black Box Programme
and the
Rose Gold Flame as Antidote

How to shield yourself from chemtrails, 5G, EMFs and other energetic warfare through alchemical unification

Magenta Pixie

This book is dedicated to all the truth seekers and healers of the world.

May you be blessed with the love of the rose gold flame as you walk the path of 'activated phirc', extinguishing the flames of destruction and fanning the flames that are creation itself.

Your heart and my heart, we beat as one with the heartbeat of our mother Gaia.

Contents

It's not my brothers and sisters to blame,

But corrupted code within the game.

Although it's known by many a name,

I see the antidote is a rose gold flame.

Magenta Pixie

Introduction

This transmission from 'the Nine' is presented in response to questions regarding vaccines, chemtrails, EMFs, 5G and disharmonies/infighting within the truth and spiritual communities.

Utilising the 'Krystal river' (Schumann resonance) through the 'rose gold flame' as antidote. Discernment tools are also provided.

1: Vaccines, Chemtrails and 5G

There is much talk at the moment about vaccines and 5G. Can you speak about this?

These subjects are indeed at the forefront of the conscious minds of awakened individuals as they are both essentially 'vehicles' if you will, for the service-to-self factions to deliver that which they believe will prevent a mass awakening and thus ascension into a fifth-dimensional frequency upon planet Earth within your current timeline trajectory.

You say they are 'vehicles'. What are they transporting? What are they delivering?

They deliver substances, in different ways. Vaccines being biological, and the scrambled signal you call '5G' being electrical and magnetic waves, that prevent mass awakening. The theory from the service-to-self perspective is that critical mass will be prevented, as in the correct critical mass point needed to affect change within your planetary and thus galactic environment. As in, those that 'bypass' or are 'immune from' the transported substances will not be enough individuals in number to create critical mass.

Are they correct?

Their theory holds merit based on the information they have. Let us just say that their calculations regarding critical mass are incorrect. The premise they base their theory on is incorrect, not the theory itself.

So are you saying that they will not achieve their goal? That critical mass will be reached?

In your most probable timeline trajectory, critical mass needed to affect change within your planetary and thus galactic environment has already been reached.

So does this mean that vaccines and 5G, or rather their use as vehicles, are no threat to the starseeds or the ascension itself?

Potentially this is what it means. Let us explain further.

There are many issues at play here and that which you ask us is multidimensional and multifaceted, therefore we aim to break this down.

Let us for example take vaccines. Without presenting the long historical, medical discoveries and journeys that have taken place within the quantum history of your Earth, let us just say that the original theories and aims for global vaccination were coming from positive thought processes with population healing rather than harm as the original seed point. However, the original premise the theory was based on was an incorrect one. We refer here to germs, viruses, bacteria and other mechanisms within the human body that were, and still are, not understood. Those that held the very first theories regarding vaccination were 'walking in the dark' if you will, yet their intentions were positive.

The vaccination programme itself was then hijacked as almost all systems are, or have been in your planet's past. This is no longer so but that is another subject, another transmission.

The hijacking created the global vaccine programme's agenda from one of healing to one of, ultimately, control through deliberate interference of natural growth on many levels within the human body. However, what adds to the confusion regarding vaccines themselves is the fact that some of the original creators of the global vaccine programme were coming from genuine intention to heal, wipe out disease and save lives. Whereas other creators were service-to-self agents coming from the need to control and halt evolution. The hijacking is almost never complete. Always leaving the genuine and positive within the hijacked system creating a multi-levelled intentional process, seed points from both positive and negative polarities which retains confusion and creates a series of false screens throughout the hijacked project or system.

The false screens remain, although dissemination and dissecting of those false screens has now started to take place.

13

There is much more we could say on this subject but you have asked us several questions, so we aim to respond to each of them within this transmission.

The global vaccine programme, as a hijacked system, added to the signal, beacon or call that reverberated throughout your cosmic space/time sector and was responded to. Starseeds began to incarnate in their droves in response to this call. The vaccine programme was only one part of the call, there were many other hijacked systems creating their own signals and beacons that were also heard.

There were starseeds that incarnated in order to experience, let us call this 'vaccine damage' as this pushed the evolutionary awareness and energies into the desire for true healing and more understanding regarding how your human system works. There were starseeds that incarnated in order to overcome the 'vaccine damage' so they may become true master healers and all that this entails.

There were starseeds who incarnated to flourish as totally vaccine-free, living incarnation experiences leading to yet more knowledge and expansion. As we have said, this is a multifaceted subject.

Your question is specific to vaccines being a threat to the starseeds and to ascension.

Ultimately, no, vaccines are not a threat to the starseed network as a whole and certainly not to ascension itself. The original seed point intention from the hijackers has ultimately failed and at this point during that time period, which we may call 'their last stand', they are holding tight to their agendas and hijacked systems with renewed vigour. This, however, flips into an opposing manifestation. For the spiritual phrase "What you resist persists" is most accurate.

However, there are still starseeds vulnerable to the toxins that vaccines carry and/or to the physical reactions within the body that occur through their use. Still there are starseeds in incarnation that have made choices to experience the resulting 'vaccine damage', not for their own choice necessarily but, through the indigo revolution and rising, the teaching of others through experience and example. Within other starseed incarnations are the informed decisions made to detox and heal from vaccine damage and to live a vaccine-free lifestyle.

Whilst we say vaccines ultimately will not stop the ascension process and are not a threat, we are not endorsing their use. We are simply saying that the starseed awareness and light has created a new pathway as is in accordance with synchronicity and the synergy with natural forces and laws.

Therefore, to hear our words and interpret that vaccines are safe is incorrect. So too is it incorrect to hear our words and interpret that they are a global threat to humanity and to your planetary ascension.

The result of vaccine damage is created by the interaction between you as an organism and your environment. Vaccines are part of that environment within your current timeline trajectory, despite being a hijacked system.

Therefore, your interaction with vaccines per se will be based on your knowledge, your pre-incarnate blueprint or past life contracts (known also as 'fate' or 'destiny').

When it comes to the healing and detoxification of substances within the body carried in as a 'Trojan horse' through the global vaccination programme, we would ask you to look twofold. One to the physical body itself such as foods, liquids, herbs and other high level, high vibratory substances which can lock onto the harmful substances and chelate them from the body, and also to the movement of the body itself which creates energetic flow also adding to detoxification pathways. It would be easy to say 'nutrition' and 'exercise', yet it goes much further than this and third-dimensional interpretations of nutrition and exercise are not necessarily enough for the detoxification, chelation and flow that we speak of. It is more in alignment to say 'conscious, aware nutrition and bodily movement creating energetic flow within cohesive pattern', in order to give a fuller picture of what is needed here.

The second part of healing and detoxification will be to look to the spiritual body or energy system and work with the matrix awareness, matrix mastery, creating the energetic firewalls and immunities needed to 'unplug' from the hijacked systems and connect to the natural order, rhythm and flow of your planet and universe.

This can be done through many pathways, systems, models and teachings. Ultimately your alignment and resonance through the higher heart leads the way in this. If synchronicity is in your life, then you are indeed on that path and in that moment of synchronicity you are unplugged from the hijacked system. The more you walk that path, the more time you spend there, the more you free yourself from that control. However one must come back into the third-dimensional system in order to integrate and anchor the physical body itself.

Healing is a beautiful journey and leads naturally to the awareness of the higher dimensions, for your release of physical and energetic toxicity leads to a lightness of spirit that takes you into the realms of light and spirit. Indeed you become light and spirit.

We respond now to the second part of your question which is regarding the scrambled signal you call '5G'.

Whilst the intentions for this 5G are similar, in themselves, to the global vaccine programme, the implementation is very different. The service-to-self factions have had, shall we say 'difficulty', in the implementation of this.

The seed point intention for this was never coming from the positive, as was the case for vaccines originally. The seed point for an electrical, magnetic, low dense pulse as a field, was always to scramble the natural magnetic fields of the human body, or rather the connection between the Earth's magnetic fields and the human body's fields as a means of control and prevention of activation of DNA. Chemicals (in the form of chemtrails, pesticides, clothing, bedding, cosmetics and so on) were the first part of this programme and the electrical fields are the second part. This is a warfare type programme, created many years ago upon your planet with a stage by stage implementation. The idea was to have full cooperation and ultimately demand for this system. The cooperation for and demand for the system has proceeded as was intended, apart from the minority few that have remained aware throughout or become aware during the implementation of the programme.

We shall call this programme, involving chemical and electrical/magnetic disrupters of the natural organic field, the 'black box programme'. We give it this name due to your global memories and knowings collectively triggered into an intrinsic understanding of this programme.

One aspect of this programme, in order for it to work in its fullest, was to use 'inverse magic', known to you also as 'black magic' or 'dark magic'. This, in its simplest form, was to create and harness negative emotion in order to 'power-up' the black box programme. Meaning the power itself, for the black box programme to actually work on a global scale, would come from the people of Earth. From humanity itself.

The global vaccine programme did not need the addition of inverse magic. It used instead chaos or confusion magic, by leaving positive intention alongside negative intention within the creation of the vaccine programme.

That confusion was not available to the service-to-self factions, for the black box programme as the full intentional seed points for the programme were all from the negative polarity. Therefore - and this is most important - creating the fear of the programme itself was, essentially, the greater part of the programme.

We repeat, *creating the fear of the programme itself was, essentially, the greater part of the programme.*

As in, fear of the chemicals, through programmes such as chemtrail release and fear of the 5G network. We are not saying that the chemicals and the scrambled electrical field signals are not harmful, it is important for you to understand that we are not saying this.

What we are saying is that fear of an outside system, a hijacked system, weakens your own spiritual biological network and creates that which you hold fear of. It gives power to it. It also takes you away from your understanding and awareness of your own intrinsic power and, most importantly, your collective power.

As we have said, the starseeds have already reached critical mass to the level needed to affect change. You already hold that collective power. That collective power becomes an entity, or collective of entities, in its own right. This force, an extraterrestrial force, is able to enact change on your behalf.

So when we say to you 'the extraterrestrials of light will not allow global destruction of any kind', you will understand what we mean.

In this case, 'the extraterrestrials' we refer to are your collective power, taking on its own intelligence and consciousness.

So this will go some way to explaining what we mean when we say that the service-to-self factions have had difficulties implementing the 5G scrambled field. Things have not worked out in the way they had intended and envisaged. This was and is the same with the chemical Trojan horse programme, the other part of that which we are calling 'the black box programme'.

We could say that 'extraterrestrials' have prevented and blocked implementation of these programmes. We could also say 'the collective power of the starseed consciousness' has affected reality and prevented or blocked implementation of the programme. Both would be accurate as both are essentially (not completely) the same thing.

So are we saying attempts to implement the 5G network upon your planet have already been made? Yes, this is what we are saying.

Have these attempts been blocked or thwarted?

Yes, they have, in the form that the service-to-self factions originally hoped for. A 'smaller' or 'watered-down' version has been implemented as a 'test' form, or trials have been carried out in very remote locations on your planet.

So will 5G be implemented and is it a threat to starseeds?

There are several possibilities looking at the various potentials that branch off into different 'mini trajectories' if you will, from your timeline:

1) The implementation of 5G in the form originally intended by service-to-self groups causing widespread issues within the planetary ecosystem and human body and thus preventing ascension into the fifth dimension.

This potential, although it exists as a branch within the overall probability field, is extremely unlikely. It is, in actuality, not possible for this potential to manifest within your current probable trajectory. We say 'extremely unlikely' only because:

a) There are no absolutes in reality creation, and

b) The awareness of this potential within service-to-self and some service-to-others thought field processes creates the 'branch' within the overall probability field.

However, that 'branch' is inactive or 'dormant' if you will. It holds no charge or cohesion with which to create probability in physicality.

So why is this extremely unlikely (or not possible)? The 'extraterrestrials' or 'starseed collective consciousness' will simply not allow damage at that level as the negative polarity field far outweighs the positive polarity field.

The service-to-self groups wish to 'master nature', as in *change the very laws of nature itself.* This creates a consequence or a new 'cosmic purpose' if you will, that flips the balance back to equal polarity. It is simply not possible, in your current timeline, to master the laws of nature through controlling them or changing them. The only way one can master the laws of nature is by 'going with the flow' with them, or merging with them (becoming unified with them).

Even if this extremely unlikely probability were to unfold and manifest, a new probability branch would be created as a response to this in order to remain within probability balance. Therefore this exact scenario becoming actuality, and remaining so, would not occur.

Another way of looking at this would be to say that if this probability did occur, it would occur upon one timeline and the majority of individuals upon Earth would 'jump' to another timeline where they do not experience this occurrence.

The laws of nature are complex, ever-changing, multidimensional and quantum. The service-to-self groups, aware of the quantum nature of the universe, do try to account for the different potentials. Yet this is like playing chess with a master chess player that can never be beaten. The reason being is that the chess player is a innocent child, allowing pure guidance and flow to influence his moves within the chess game. The service-to-self groups use chaos, demand and subterfuge which works only to the level of polarity balance and cannot go beyond that.

Therefore, the service-to-self groups only have a certain bandwidth in which to work. This 'restriction' within their quest to master the laws of nature, bleeds over into all their projects with a fully negative seed intention such as the black box programme.

2) The implementation of 5G in the form originally intended without causing any disruption or harm to the environment or the human body.

Some individuals could potentially create this timeline for themselves. However, we are looking at the critical mass field potential which is experienced by the majority collective consciousness of humanity on Earth.

The original intention for energetic warfare, and thus prevention of critical mass awareness, is tied up as a black box pattern within the intentions for the original 5G pattern. This could potentially be 'backtracked' to a 'changed' seed point, as in, trace the timeline back to its origin and jump to the start of a new timeline. If you were to do this, the new seed point to that timeline would not be a black box programme. You would find the service-to-self polarity itself and subsequent inverted matrix programmes, absent from the continuing new timeline. This would ultimately be a total jump to a non-polarity, non-free will universe. The concept of backtracking within timelines is beyond the scope of this transmission. What we present here is that the original 5G pattern within your current reality experience holds potential for harm to individuals and environment. We only mention option two as a potential as it exists as a 'branch' within that overall probability field with activation for some individuals. You each experience different timelines depending on your seed point intentions within your thought field processes and the resulting geometric presentations you hold within your paradigms.

Due to original 5G pattern holding potential for harm and environment for the majority collective consciousness, then we conclude that 5G in its original form is extremely unlikely to manifest in any timeline experienced by humanity on Earth on a collective level. Those who may move into this potential are the individuals who would align with probability two and would therefore experience no harm to themselves or to their environment in that reality. From the majority collective consciousness perspective, we would call this an 'alternate' reality (explanation of which is outside the scope of this transmission).

3) The implementation of 5G in a 'watered-down' form. Still causing a scrambling and disruption of the environment and human body but not to the degree that the original 5G form would have caused.

More likely to occur than the previous two scenarios but still a low probability. As although this would keep the polarities in balance, it would still affect ascension itself and the ecosystem of Earth, including many human individuals, holding back their growth and spiritual evolution.

This is not the desire of planet Earth herself, given the fact that she is a planet that is nearing completion (a whole other transmission).

4) The implementation of 5G in a 'watered-down' form causing scrambling and disruption to parts of the environment and to the human body in varying degrees, with an antidote to both.

This is a much more likely scenario with a fairly high probability.

5) 5G not being implemented at all, and this aspect to the black box programme being scrapped altogether.

This is also a scenario that we would say is a 'branch' within the polarity field that holds activation potential. There is a reasonable balance of probability that this could manifest (neither a high nor a low probability) specifically as a 'bleed-through' into probability four (creating a sixth probability, which is a combination of probability four and five).

Presenting what is actually the most likely scenario for your planet at this given nexus point/now moment in time, is that probability 5 and probability 4 both occur together.

Now if any probability has been 'seen' or 'viewed', it will come into play in some form with each probability collapsing as a field and imploding into one another. Meaning 'pieces' of each probability could occur creating a new probability that holds manifestation templates for all the probabilities. As we have said, this is extremely complex and convoluted and for the third-dimensional brain to decode or break this down, it is quite a challenge.

We will therefore present the imploding timelines as one linear probability, which is the highest probability for your planet at the point of the now moment that is the downloading of this monadic transmission.

The most likely probability is that aspects of probability 5 occur, meaning 5G cannot be implemented. This is most likely to manifest as all sorts of problems or challenges as in 'things not working' or 'things going wrong'.

Then imploding into this probability will be the template that is probability 4. The implementation of 5G in a 'watered-down' form, causing scrambling and disruption to parts of the environment and to the human body in varying degrees with an antidote to both.

If probability 4 then manifests as actuality (with a bleed-through from probability 5), then what you are looking at is a fluctuating system, taking on a life of its own beyond that of its creator.

The black box programme itself is built with artificial intelligences in mind, and that part of manifestation cannot be controlled. For any intelligent consciousness, including artificial intelligence, can develop its own thought processes creating a 'walk-in' type of experience (as in a form of free will, even within a restricted probability field). This would make the actual manifestation of the black box programme and 5G an 'unknown quantity', even to the creators.

We could take for example, your moon. This was originally an 'artificial' construct if you will, compared to the natural organic 'birthing' of the other planetary bodies within your solar system. Yet over many millennia, your moon gained a 'walk-in' consciousness and now stands as an organic planetary body, despite her origins and history. She (the moon) has consciousness.

So regarding 5G as a scrambled signal network, what is the antidote?

The antidote, of course, is you!

The collective consciousness of the starseeds we spoke of (which we refer to as the 'Divine Princess Aurora' - for many reasons, one being that that is her name!), which is an extraterrestrial consciousness, is an antidote. It stands as 'pure potential', allowing you to change a manifested timeline or timeline jump from a current timeline into a new one.

This aspect of extraterrestrial consciousness will 'not allow' widespread global damage to the ecosystem of your planet or to your human bodies.

If any 'threat' comes into your planetary system that looks like it could, as a cosmic virus, affect life on a grand scale, then there will ALWAYS be an antidote.

We repeat, *there will ALWAYS be an antidote.*

The antidote, in this respect, for this particular aspect of the black box programme is the 'heartbeat' of your planet Earth. The unconditional love and nurturing of your mother Gaia. This heartbeat or planetary nurturing that we speak of, you may know as the 'Schumann resonance'.

2: The Schumann Resonance as Black Box Antidote

So how is the Schumann resonance the antidote to the black box programme? (Chemicals released into the environment and 5G)

The Schumann resonance is a continuous tone or beat (in truth, a frequency) of your planet Earth. It is an energetic pulse (like a heartbeat).

Out in the cosmos, if you could 'hear' planet Earth's heartbeat, it would be a musical note, played in harmony with all the other planetary musical notes.

It is not just planetary bodies that have musical notes, all 'space debris' and 'cosmic bodies' have musical notes. The universe is indeed a most 'noisy' place. Although, when organic and natural, the 'noise' is as the most beautiful piece of music you could ever imagine - known also as 'the music of the spheres'.

Each musical note is a frequency (an electromagnetic pulse) that, as a 'tuning fork', gives life to the inhabitants and the ecosystems that exist upon its planetary body.

The incarnated humans upon planet Earth are constantly being 'retuned' by what you know as the 'Schumann resonance'. An etherisation takes place. The matter and antimatter aspects of the human energy system are constantly in a state of exchange. Matter (blood and bone) and antimatter (ethereal energy, chi, Kundalini phire, cosmic ambrosia, manna, ormus) 'exchange places' if you will.

In truth, the blood and bone transforms or alchemises into the cosmic ambrosia and vice versa. This is also known as 'taking energy from the cosmos through the crown chakra' and 'anchoring energy from the Earth through the base chakra/soles of the feet'. It is a constant flowing state whereby the matter and antimatter systems of the body are synergistically intertwined, in a relationship.

One could also say the sacred masculine and the divine feminine move into an inner 'divine marriage' or 'alchemical merge'.

This creates a 'third' entity or expression. This is the way energy works when following a creational life blueprint. This blueprint is known as 'the Holy Trinity' or 'sacred trine' or 'the cosmic triad'.

We could also liken this to frequency through colour (light, simply a different manifestation of the Schumann resonance fields than that of sound). So silver would be the divine feminine, gold would be the divine masculine and the 'rose gold' would be the child or the creation.

The rose gold is the manifestation of inner alchemy or divine marriage.

It is the Schumann resonance (heartbeat of the Earth) that synchronises with the energetic frequency (heartbeat) of the human being.

These subtle energetics of sound/light manifestation are at play all the time, in the environment and in the human body.

The 'rose gold' (as in a 'ray' or a 'flame') is the creational result (or birth) of the dance between the gold and silver (matter and antimatter). The Schumann resonance is the conductor and the material essence of that dance. It may be the heartbeat of the planet but so too is it the 'lifeblood' for the human being.

Every human, animal, plant holds this 'lifeblood' (the synergistic energy flow that is Earth's Schumann resonance).

If you were to imagine the Schumann resonance as perhaps a body of water rather than a musical tone or beat, this is also helpful for explanation. It is, indeed, an etheric river (we call this the 'Krystal river') and it flows up through the soles of the feet of the individual (from the Earth) and down through the head of the individual, the crown chakra (from the cosmos).

The Schumann resonance is a unified field if you view it in its whole form. As an aspect or 'part of', then it is an individual beat/tone/pulse but in its unified whole form it is a Krystal river of antimatter liquid light that flows through you (as a human being incarnated on Earth) and through all life on Earth. It then joins with the other Krystal rivers of liquid light within all the other planetary bodies in your solar system (and beyond), changing its beat and form to flow in alignment with the 'Schumann resonance' of each planetary body, satellite, star or indeed space debris.

Or indeed, this is how it works within a healthy planetary body and healthy solar system.

This beat or pulse that is part of a greater unified field of oscillating waves, known as 'the voice of Terra', (your planet Earth) keeps you in incarnation, grounded and anchored within your physical bodies.

The Krystal river, antimatter/matter flow within your own body, connects into the mitochondria within your cells, flooding it with a 'charge' (like charging a battery). This is what gives you energy.

When you move into spiritual discipline within your lives and 'raise the Kundalini', you are simply activating a 'higher charge' if you will, within the cell mitochondria. Then, through a photosynthesis type of process, you transform the carbon-based atoms into silicate-based atoms. This is an intricate and complex process and one you may know as 'DNA activation' or 'light body transformation'.

Our aim here is to present to you the interconnectedness of your physical systems and energy body so that you may understand how the Schumann resonance is the antidote to black box technology and how to connect with it (the Schumann resonance) or consciously anchor yourself to it so that you may utilise it for healing, balance, rejuvenation and ultimately ascension. In the process, this also becomes a 'shield' from black box programme technologies.

Remember, the Krystal river within your body is a living force. It is a living intelligence that, through projection of itself (utilising plasmic forms) it creates substance that manifests in your reality as reality itself.

Now we mentioned that this earthly and cosmic synergistic flow is how it works within a healthy planetary body and healthy solar system. As you are aware (if you have found your way to and are listening to/reading this material), there has been hijacking of healthy organic systems upon your planet. This does not mean that healthy systems and energy flows have been destroyed (that would cease life as you know it altogether), but it has been 'slowed down' or 'blocked' in places and for some individuals.

Let us imagine that there is a barrier that keeps all hijacked systems within a certain radius and when you 'break free from' or 'break through' the barrier, you are no longer subject to the hijacked systems.

This is what has happened. A great many individuals have broken free from the barrier and are no longer confined to operating within the restricted radius holding hijacked systems. They have broken free into an abundant and infinite realm of organic and natural structure.

These individuals (we call them 'starseeds') have been able to access a 'greater stream' shall we say, within that Krystal river of liquid light that is the Schumann resonance.

Within the restricted radius of hijacked systems is enough Krystal river, liquid light (Schumann resonance) to keep you alive and functioning - although not in optimum capacity. Let us say that here, you are accessing one stream of that liquid light.

When you break free from the barrier and are no longer subject to the limitations of hijacked systems, you access multiple streams of liquid light.

25

The Krystal river becomes, for you, an entire network of Krystal rivers joining together.

Let us look at this in terms of mitochondrial nourishment and energy.

On the one stream bandwidth, the mitochondria receives enough charge to stay alive. The liquid plasma remains at a carbon-based level, rejuvenating that carbon in a recyclable fashion that cleanses it and gives it life force. But it remains within its same energetic form. The higher charge (plasmic phire) needed for transformation is not available.

On the multiple stream bandwidth, the mitochondria receives the higher charge. The liquid plasma begins to oscillate at the frequency level known as the 'golden mean equation' or the mathematical 'Fibonacci sequence'. It begins to create an ambrosiac liquid plasmic light or what you may know as 'white powder gold' or 'ormus'. The liquid plasma light oscillates at faster and faster levels of this quantum Fibonacci sequence and it creates a holographic image of itself moving in a triple sine wave weave pattern or triple spiral movement (rather than a cyclical pattern).

The carbon molecule then begins to transform due to the extreme high frequencies and spin speed of the oscillating liquid plasma. Like two pieces of flint rubbing together, it creates a fire. The carbon molecule alchemises into a silicate molecule. This is what is meant by changing from carbon-based DNA to crystalline-based DNA.

When this happens within the human structure, the liquid plasmic light spirals in this triple weave formation up through the body and over the head, flooding the pineal gland with the silicate, crystalline substance.

The little tiny diamond-like clusters inside the pineal begin to radiate 'complete holographic versions of themselves' and like a cinema projector, they beam blueprints (created by your cohesive thought and matching emotion) into the antimatter reality. They sit there as a geometric pre-matter form before spiralling into the physical dimension themselves as their absolute match in matter.

When critical mass was reached amongst the individuals who all broke free from the restricted radius within the barrier and alchemised their mitochondrial charge all at the same time, their collective emotional desires and matching cohesive thought patterns began to create a new reality and shape a new world.

Many different inverted matrix, black box technologies were created to prevent too many individuals from breaking through the barrier and preventing critical mass. However, as we said in the earlier part of this transmission, the premise regarding critical mass creation was an incorrect one.

It is not the *amount* of individuals that create critical mass, it is the level of liquid plasma they are able to radiate together that creates critical mass.

We repeat... *it is not the <u>amount</u> of individuals that create critical mass, it is the level of liquid plasma they are able to radiate together that creates critical mass.*

It takes a far smaller group of individuals to create the critical mass radiation needed than was estimated by those creating the black box programme technologies and inverted matrix systems.

Mass is created by light (as in volume, strength, brilliance, loudness and so on), not numbers of individuals. However, a group of individuals are needed to do this (as opposed to one), but far less than was originally estimated.

Each individual bounces off the resonance of the other if the oscillating fields within their mitochondrial ormus-filled cells are of a mathematically resonant match (a like vibration). The more individuals that radiate this plasmic light, the more that other individuals can break free from the restricted barrier as plasmic light is not confined to one space and time.

When soul groups incarnate together in large clusters (like starseeds) and one 'aspect' of their soul becomes flooded with plasmic light, then the genetic/soul connected blood (within the other aspect of their soul) also becomes flooded with plasmic light (if conditions allow for that, such as trauma release and integration). This means that many human individuals break free from this barrier at the same time. Critical mass gets stronger and stronger and their reach gets wider and wider. They begin to influence the entire probability field.

The dark magical tricks and methods of the service-to-self groups, that have influenced the probability field for aeons, begin to lose their power as the plasmic light of the starseeds (immune from inverted matrix barriers) has a wider reach and a higher power.

The black box programme was intended to 'cast a wider net' if you will. Literally. First a chemical net and then an electromagnetic frequency net using an electrical field with output at a higher level than that of the Schumann resonance.

The intention was that the activated starseeds would be 'caught in the wider net' and this would stop the critical mass influence on the probability fields for Earth.

You see, the mitochondria that has transformed into silicate molecular structure and the pineal gland that is flooded with plasmic light, are antennas.

The electromagnetic field would act as a 'false Krystal river' as in a *false Schumann resonance.* The aim was that the antennas of those with the crystalline frequency (silicate mitochondrial molecular structure) would broadcast and connect to the higher ranges of the false Schumann resonance, 5G, scrambling the signal for the activated one and pulling apart the strong collective consciousness that is manifesting a positive and higher polarity for Earth.

What is now happening within the starseed collective is a growing awareness of the 5G implementation. The service-to-self factions have continued to utilise chaos factors through fear-based emotion regarding the 5G network, the same way they manipulated the population into fear regarding 'swine flu' or 'bird flu' when previous black box programmes were created.

The antidotes were an automatic and organic response to the swine flu and bird flu programmes. Fear reactions were relied on heavily and also the roll-out of the medication to supposedly cure and prevent the swine/bird flu was also part of that black box programme.

The starseeds now, when realising the collective power they have when they 'act together', are in the process of neutralising the 5G network. Hence the reason why the original form of the intended 5G is extremely unlikely to manifest. It is the watered-down version of 5G that is the higher probability. This watered-down version does not have the ability to match the output frequency of the Schumann resonance.

However, in order to counteract any possible influence from the scrambled signal of the watered-down 5G field, the starseeds are collectively (both consciously and unconsciously) raising the frequency of the Schumann resonance. Remembering that the Schumann resonance is part of that overall Krystal river and the awakened and activated starseeds are part of that. When they become silicate connected (crystalline) instead of carbon, then the Schumann resonance raises higher and higher in its frequency.

Is it the Schumann resonance activating the starseeds, or is it their raise in consciousness that is raising the Schumann resonance?

It is both. This is happening in perfect synchronisation with one another. The Schumann resonance is one part of the Krystal river and the silicate molecular structure of the starseeds is the other part of the Krystal river. The projected image beams into antimatter and the resulting manifestation in matter is the other part of the Krystal river. It is a unified field and a trinity field.

So if/when the watered-down 5G scrambled field is implemented, as long as the Schumann resonance is 'higher' in its frequency than the 5G signal, then the antennas within the starseed's blood, bone, mitochondria, neurotransmitters and entire endocrine system will 'connect to' and 'engage'/'exchange'/'merge with' the Schumann resonance, Krystal river rather than the false signal of 5G.

This does not necessarily show itself within scientific measurements or scale. The Schumann resonance may look to some as if it has not changed in hundreds of years, depending on technology used and interpretation of the mathematical measurements involved.

Other technologies show clearly the increase in the Schumann resonance frequency, yet even these do not show completely accurately the measurements. The only technology to accurately record the Schumann resonance is the organic, crystalline activated technology within the starseeds themselves. Although crystal dowsing can be most effective as can experimentation with salt water, magnets and compasses.

The starseeds can *feel* when the Schumann resonance is peaking. There are spikes within the Schumann resonance that fluctuate in synergistic resonance and synchronisation with the collective consciousness of the starseeds (the individuals with the silicate mitochondrial charge).

So the way forward for the starseeds, if they wish to know how to continue to bypass inverted system black box programmes and directly key into the natural, organic, harmonious frequency pulse of the Earth, is to 'tune their antennae' in the direction of the Schumann resonance. As we have said, the Schumann resonance is the antidote.

How do the starseeds do this?

There are several ways this can be done. We present to you the shielding technique utilising the rose gold flame.

The rose gold flame (or ray) is an actual fire that is created within the human body as silicate becomes the charge for mitochondria instead of carbon. The gold (male) and silver (female) marry together, creating the rose gold (the triad point, Holy Trinity or Merkabah activation).

The activation of the Merkabah is beyond the scope of this transmission, but know that the rose gold flame is a Merkabah activation in itself.

There are other ways to connect into the Schumann resonance and not only utilise its rhythm and beat as a frequency shield, but also for creation itself through the holographic blueprint projections broadcast and beamed from the activated crystalline pineal gland.

We shall move, in this transmission, to the practical applications for starseeds wanting to tune their antennas to the organic heartbeat of Gaia and not to the false inverted matrix through black box programme technology.

We shall introduce you to the rose gold flame and the shielding process. Before we do this, we respond to your question regarding disharmony and infighting within the truth movement and spiritual communities.

3: Something Rotten in the State of Denmark *

* "Something is rotten in the state of Denmark", a line from the play *Hamlet* by William Shakespeare. It is often used in modern parlance to describe corruption or a situation in which something appears to be deeply wrong.

It seems many 'wayshowers', as in 'leaders in the movement' (lightworkers, truth seekers and teachers), are against each other. Why is this and is this going to be counterproductive to the unity we need as starseeds? Are some of these individuals actually controlled opposition?

It is correct that there is what you may call 'infighting' within the truth movement and spiritual communities.

Within the spiritually aware individuals, every disagreement between them minimally affects the overall energetic consciousness due to forgiveness, acceptance and surrender being part of the overall energetic make-up of the aware and activated individuals.

However, within the truth movement there is a much 'wider range' of activation and it is the *level of activation* that determines the resonance each individual feels with another.

Some of the truth movement teachers are spiritually activated, as in all the chakras are in alignment and the DNA sequencing is moving in alignment with the starseed consciousness, even if that individual is essentially a teacher within the truth movement when it comes to subject matter within their teaching.

Other truth movement teachers have activated certain aspects of self yet are still broadcasting within a predominantly third-dimensional and fourth-dimensional consciousness. The overall starseed consciousness is fifth-dimensional.

However, there are also those who are able to access fifth-dimensional consciousness in part, yet due to unresolved traumas within their system they are somewhat fragmented and they also do not stand in full alignment with the overall collective consciousness of the starseeds.

This overall collective consciousness is a consciousness that holds individualised intelligence, energy and the perspective of a self-realised or individualised entity. We refer to this feminine entity as the 'Divine Princess Aurora'.

Let us explain further.

We can use the chakra system and the dimensional scale to explain different levels of awakening. We could also use a simplified model that also stands as accurate descriptive presentation of the DNA. This is but one model.

The model we shall use here in this transmission is that of the Holy Trinity, cosmic triad or divine trine. There are many interpretations of this. For example, your symbol known as the Celtic knot 'triquetra'.

This would also be known as trilocational consciousness or the triple helix as opposed to the double helix. This is the level of awareness that the Divine Princess Aurora holds. This is the level of awareness within the awakening starseed collective consciousness.

It is the case that there are individuals who have moved beyond this level of activation into sixth/seventh and above dimensional scale consciousness and 'beyond the triple helix' into infinite helix (multilocational consciousness into omnipresence) activation. We are remaining with the current predominant level of awakening within the starseed consciousness for this transmission which is the triple helix/trilocational.

This is a layered quantum memory awakening within an individual. This is the movement from the carbon-based molecular structure into the silicate/crystalline-based molecular structure or light body.

Within your truth movement and spiritual communities you have individuals who have, if you will, 'activated' one part of this trinity, or two parts, or all three. Remember this is one model used to explain activation.

We present each part of this trinity as a '33 and one third' expression of one unit. We could say that the activation of one 33 and one third unit is akin to the third-dimensional consciousness. Two 33 and one third units is akin to the fourth-dimensional consciousness and all three 33 and one third units is akin to the fifth-dimensional consciousness and completes the trinity.

This is a very basic model of the DNA layered activation as it moves in mirrored, replicated form. It replicates itself as in the 'matter aspect' of the DNA molecule, which is then replicated within the antimatter aspect.

So one 33 and one third unit is matter.

Two 33 and one third units are branching into antimatter.

Three 33 and one third units have created a fully realised geometric pattern within matter and antimatter, creating a marriage or merge.

We use this simplified DNA activation model now to explain what is occurring within your truth movement and spiritual communities. This will assist you within your own discernment when you make evaluations and analysis of the teachings and information you receive when you follow or research these individuals.

Firstly, may we say that every starseed who begins to activate this trinity we speak of is a potential leader or teacher within this movement. Even those who only hold one 33 and one third unit within the trinity. These individuals are able to access high intelligence and think critically. They will have highly activated third eye chakras or perhaps the solar plexus is activated. Although they do not stand in full balance as a complete trinity, they can still bring their perspective to the table.

So what we are saying here is that every starseed has the ability to teach. This does not mean they have all the answers or that the premise they base their conclusion on is accurate. However, they are able to share their perspective and each teacher *will* hold some level of accuracy.

When 'everyone becomes a teacher' or 'everyone is an expert', this can be very confusing and chaotic for a society. However, this is the way it works when mass activation takes place on a global scale. Finding order within that chaos is for the seeker - you, each starseed as they find their way and walk their chosen path. Each seeker is the student of the way. At the same time each seeker, as an activated individual, is also ready to teach. Therefore when you listen to your teachers, know they are also seekers. They are also students.

When an individual activates the three 33 and one third units and completes the trinity, they then hold a level of mastery within that teaching. Yet they remain even more the seeker than before. You will have heard the phrase:

"The more you know, the more you realise how much there is to learn."

This is most accurate when it comes to your individual awakening.

So let us look at the energetic patterns within your current truth movement and spiritual communities, and those that stand as the leaders and teachers within.

This will explain to you the infighting and the contradictions you may be faced with as a seeker or investigative researcher in this field. This will thus give you tools through information in order to aid you with your own discernment.

Let us take, for example, two individuals that stand as leaders within the truth movement. Let us imagine that these two individuals have activated all three 33 and one third units within their DNA and hold the triple helix, trinity field. These individuals would therefore be standing as spiritual teachers as well as leaders within the truth movement, even if they do not present as such.

Let us say that these two individuals are closely aligned with a third individual who has only activated two 33 and one third units within his/her trinity field, due to unresolved and buried trauma. If trauma is not integrated then this will prevent the full trinity being formed, using the trinity model we present here.

These three individuals present their work together as leaders and teachers within the truth movement, branching into the spiritual leadership movement in varying degrees. We use fictional examples here based on accurate starseed consciousness energetics.

Let us say that these three individuals are two men and one woman. We shall call them Peter, Paul and Charlotte.

Now let us also say that there are three other individuals as leaders within the truth movement. These individuals are also two men and one woman. We shall call these individuals John, Steven and Mary. These individuals also work together yet all three have only activated one 33 and one third unit within their overall trinity DNA field. They operate within third-dimensional consciousness yet have high intelligence, good critical thinking skills and are able to put together a well presented teaching. Their teaching holds accurate information. However, many of the premises used within their constructed arguments or discussions are based on third-dimensional structures and all constructed arguments and presented discussions within the teaching will be interpreted third-dimensionally.

This is not a fault or a criticism. It is simply as it is.

Let us say that Charlotte, the truth leader and spiritual teacher who holds unresolved trauma within her fields and has only activated two 33 and one third units within her trinity field, presents a teaching. Let us say that much of this teaching is accurate yet some of the teaching is distortion based on the imbalance within the trinity construction caused by the unresolved trauma.

This again is not wrong. It is not a criticism. It is simply as it is. Let us say this person's heart is open, she is full of compassion and love and is not fully consciously aware of the distortion she presents in her teaching. Let us say that Peter and Paul, who both work with Charlotte, see her light and know her open heart. They absolutely embrace Charlotte as their colleague. However, Peter and Paul are both 'pure souls', as in they have all three 33 and one third units in place within their trinity field. They hold fully activated triple helix DNA formations. This does not mean that their teachings are fully accurate, however it does mean that their teachings are more likely to be accurate and hold a high level of accuracy. They will be genuine, authentic and utterly dedicated to their mission. They will have memory of their mission and know exactly what it is they have incarnated to do.

Now let us look at the other three truth leaders we mentioned. John, Steven and Mary. All three intelligent individuals with well presented teachings. These individuals have only activated one 33 and one third aspect of their trinity fields and the premise they base their critical thinking upon is a third-dimensional premise.

These three individuals witness the teachings of Charlotte. Because they have such good critical thinking skills, they are able to spot flaws in Charlotte's teachings. However because they think third-dimensionally, they do not realise that the flaws in Charlotte's teachings come from unresolved trauma. They interpret the flaws as deliberate disinformation. One of the individuals, John, believes Charlotte to be what you may know as 'controlled opposition' - as in Charlotte is a 'cabal child' or is controlled by the cabal (service-to-self factions).

John's interpretation is understandable. His critical thinking skills picked up accurate flaws within Charlotte's teachings. However, he interpreted them incorrectly and he teaches this incorrect teaching regarding Charlotte.

Every starseed holds the same mission. That of the liberation of Earth and humanity from third-dimensional reality into the 'next octave' of evolution. John is aware that part of that intrinsic starseed mission is the ending of tyranny and the bringing down of the cabal. When he sees flaws that are genuinely within Charlotte's testimony, he perceives Charlotte as a threat to his mission. He perceives her as being part of the 'opposing team' if you will.

Because John thinks third-dimensionally, he will still be experiencing and creating polarity in his life. He therefore sees Charlotte as 'the enemy'. His mission then becomes focused on discrediting Charlotte, rather than focusing on the true mission - the liberation of Earth.

John has come to a conclusion he believes to be accurate. John is not bad or wrong or evil to think of Charlotte as an 'enemy' based on his premise. Because he is third-dimensional in his thinking, despite his excellent critical thinking skills and high intelligence, he does not have all the information at hand with which to make a fully informed and accurate decision regarding Charlotte. He thinks predominantly with a subjective viewpoint. His colleagues Steven and Mary also see the flaws in Charlotte's testimony. They do not necessarily feel that Charlotte is 'controlled opposition' but they have such faith in and respect for John that they adopt his belief system. You now have three leaders in the truth movement that are focused on discrediting Charlotte, seeing her as opposing their mission and 'an enemy'.

This is then taken one step further. Because Peter and Paul work with Charlotte and embrace her as their colleague and friend, they are also seen by John, Steven and Mary as the same as Charlotte. They see all three individuals as potential 'controlled opposition' and the enemy.

Yet here we have Peter and Paul who are fully 'pure souls', having activated all three 33 and one third units within their trinity fields, and are the most likely of all these teachers to be delivering accurate and multidimensional information.

John, Steven and Mary have a great deal of followers between them. Many of these followers also follow Peter, Paul and Charlotte. Confusion sets in and disagreements occur as everyone involved moves into discernment within varying degrees.

You now have two divided camps. 'Charlotte's camp' (which includes Peter, Paul and all their followers) and 'John's camp' (which includes Steven, Mary and all their followers).

The actual truth regarding 'controlled opposition' is that, indeed, there is infiltration within the truth/lightworker communities from service-to-self factions. However, due to the natural infighting that takes place, the service-to-self factions do not need to infiltrate the movement as much as is widely believed. They sit back and watch the infighting and disagreements occur as the starseeds, in their various degrees of awakening, are 'doing their job for them'.

However, the systems on your planet are hijacked in the first place. The hijacked systems are the reasons for Charlotte's trauma and the reasons why John, Steven and Mary have only activated one 33 and one third aspect of their DNA trinity field.

Continuing with this scenario, Charlotte becomes very upset by the movement to discredit her which in turn affects Peter and Paul. They rally around each other in support, as do their followers.

This is a very simplistic presentation of how division is occurring within your truther and lightworker communities. There is infiltration from the service-to-self groups, but not to the degree that you may have been led to believe. However, we will add that service- to-self groups will try to influence some of the individual leaders in direct ways and all of the individual leaders in indirect ways.

The leaders who hold all three 33 and one third units within their trinity fields *cannot* be influenced or controlled by service-to-self groups. Because they hold a full trinity, then they are polarised positive and are immune from the effects of hijacking and infiltration.

The leaders who do not hold the full trinity activation are more susceptible to negative influence. If they hold integrity and/or insight (and these can be manifest even in a third-dimensionally thinking individual although both are, in themselves, triggers into higher activation), then these will act as barriers to infiltration regardless of trinity activation level.

We might add that there are several leaders and teachers in this field who have activated two 33 and one third units of their trinity and are actively teaching. This brings psychic insight and awareness to the individual yet this psychic insight is perceived subjectively. These teachers present truth with distortion.

The leaders/teachers that have activated all three 33 and one third units within their trinity will also have psychic insight. However, this will be perceived objectively and therefore hold less distortion and much higher accuracy.

As we have said, these characters - Peter, Paul, Charlotte, John, Steven and Mary - are *fictional* characters. They are based on *accurate* energy that is broadcast from the collective field that makes up the leaders and teachers in your truth movement and spiritual/lightworker communities.

4: Discernment and Harmony

How can we create harmony within the truth and lightworker movements? How do we discern which are the pure leaders and teachers that have activated the full trinity field within their DNA?

There already is a harmonious flow within these movements. You remember we explained how many individuals had broken free from the restricted barrier? These are the individuals who have activated all three 33 and one third units within the trinity. They have 'full units' as in they are 'in unity'. These individuals broadcast the predominant signal for the starseed collective consciousness that makes up the individualised entity 'the Divine Princess Aurora'.

From a third-dimensional perspective, one cannot 'hurry along' another individual's awakening process. Each individual must be free to awaken and activate at their own pace. The only individual that you *can* influence within this activation, is yourself. Even as a teacher or leader in the movement, you only present a perspective. If you are delivering energetic information (monadic light packages) to others through your voice, writing, art or other creations, the individual receiving those packages needs to be within receptive flow in order to receive them. Each individual is responsible for their own receptivity.

As each individual works on themselves, harmonises and balances the three 33 and one third units within their trinity fields and moves into unity, then this will create greater and greater harmony within the truth and lightworker movements.

As seekers, students or investigative researchers yourself (spiritual explorers), there are several methods needed in order to discern in balance the individual teacher or their teaching tools.

The first method is objectivity.

With every teacher or teaching tool that you utilise, view the material and the individual with objectivity. Coming from the observer viewpoint. We would include your viewing of celebrities and political leaders in the same way. Subjectivity is most necessary but it can distort your vision if you are not using simultaneous objectivity. It is the objective place that will show you the clearest view. The more you practise and utilise objectivity, the more 'DNA activation' that will take place.

Although the model of the three 33 and one third trinity into unity is a very basic model, we can point out to you that the activation of this trine occurs in a non-linear progression. This means that someone may move into full trinity unity at one point in their lives and then 'drop down' to only two units, or only one. For the purposes of this transmission, we will not explore this non-linear progression but we wish to make you aware of it.

So objectivity when observing is crucial. For this is what you are doing - observing. When you move into subjectivity and your own trauma-based issues become triggered, then you filter everything through a false premise. This happens on a global scale regarding your political leaders and it also happens, to a much lesser degree, within your truth and spiritual communities. You are responsible for your own spiritual awareness and your own discernment. Objectivity is the greatest gift you can give to yourself if you want to access the highest truth you can with very little or zero distortion.

The second method is non-judgement.

This is very akin to objectivity. You need objectivity for non-judgement as judgement is, in itself, subjective. However, there is a boundary between the two methods. Remember the example of the infighting between the two sides, 'Charlotte's camp' and 'John's camp', caused division within the truth community? Those following Charlotte (and indeed Charlotte herself) have judged John (rightly so) as attacking and discrediting Charlotte and Charlotte's work. This does not mean that John is bad, evil or even wrong, given that John has noticed genuine inconsistency in Charlotte's testimony and information. John and all his followers have judged Charlotte as deliberately misleading people for her own ends or even being 'controlled opposition'. Both these judgements have led to misinterpretation, misinformation and thus division.

To observe without judgement will give you a far clearer picture of the individual or tool in question and you will see 'layers beyond the layers' if you will. All accurate truth is multilayered.

When it comes to viewing service-to-self individuals (leaders and teachers), we understand how challenging it is for you not to judge. Yet many service-to-self individuals who deliberately mislead you have been forced, against their will, to do so. Lack of judgement does *not* mean lack of justice. Justice is created from the self and all individuals bring themselves to justice ultimately. Your own lack of judgement will assist you in bringing about your own fair justice and that of humanity on Earth. This brings us to the third method.

The third method is compassion.

Compassion is, in many ways, the highest emotional frequency you can hold. When it comes to viewing teachers and leaders, then objectivity and non-judgement must take precedence for they lead automatically to compassion. Compassion is extremely difficult to find when one is in subjectivity and judgement.

Compassion is, in and of itself, an extremely powerful DNA activator. Holding compassion broadcasts the matching signal of the golden mean equation or Fibonacci sequence through the cellular structure of your body, creating the molecular transformation from carbon-based to silicate/crystalline. Compassion allows flow through the trinity fields moving you from your first 33 and one third unit, into the second and then the third, bringing about full trinity and unity expression.

When viewing the teachers and leaders, holding compassion will do two things. It will assist you to observe without judgement but at the same time it will allow you to connect fully with the truth of the teacher/leader's message. We speak here of teachers and leaders within the truth and spiritual communities. Your compassion will allow you to do what is known within the spiritual communities as:

"Take what resonates and leave the rest."

This phrase is mentioned much within spiritual teachings yet it is almost impossible to implement without objectivity, non-judgement and compassion. Yet it is the single most important teaching when it comes to the receiving of another's messages and information. It is your filter.

When you listen to fully polarised, positive, full trinity activated individuals, you will not need to filter much. It is 'easy listening' if you will, especially when you hold matching frequency.

When observing a non-full trinity activated individual then one must employ the filters, which takes a little energetic work. This is the reason like-minded individuals 'follow' other like-minded teachers and leaders. It is not because they cannot think for themselves and so they need a leader, or that they need someone to follow. It is because they are in energetic resonance with that individual. This is another reason why there is division within the movements as 'like attracts like'. We could also say, "Birds of a feather flock together."

Employing these filters when observing these teachers and their work is to be done with these first three methods in place. Objectivity, non-judgement and compassion. The final and fourth method will activate your full discernment abilities and allow you to move into alignment with your inner resonation. The 'like attracts like' aspect within. That which you may know as 'the law of magnetic attraction'.

The fourth method is gratitude.

We have said to our conduit that 'gratitude is the key to life'. What we mean by this is that it activates the 'law of magnetic attraction'. Gratitude is actually the key to *creation*. It is through gratitude that you create your reality.

This is challenging to accomplish when you are observing service-to-self individuals, we understand this. Yet you do not need to hold gratitude for the individual themselves per se, or for the deeds they have done or any legacy they have left. You hold gratitude for the awareness, learning, knowledge and experience that your observation has bought to you. Holding gratitude does not mean absence of justice. Justice will always be there. You can hold compassion, non-judgement and gratitude and view everything from objectivity and still hold the desire for (or the codes for) justice within your fields and thus within your reality.

When it comes to observing the truth community leaders, speakers and spiritual teachers in your now reality, these four methods are the keys to discernment.

Objectivity, non-judgement, compassion and gratitude.

There is one clue that will let you know that your critical thinking skills and discernment are working in balance. That clue, is meaningful coincidence. What you would know as 'synchronicity'.

5: Synchronicity

Synchronicity occurs when two or more events converge together at the same time. When you are 'on the right track' in your life (as in walking the pre-incarnate blueprint, the map for your life that you created before you incarnated) then these meaningful coincidences called 'synchronicity' will occur.

You can utilise the guidance or clue of synchronicity when it comes to discernment of your spiritual teachers and truth leaders.

This occurs in ways such as:

1) You are thinking of a particular topic and then within days or even hours (sometimes within minutes), the teacher or speaker you are following puts out a creativity (book, artwork, talk, video, song, social media post or so on) that is related exactly to the topic you have been thinking about.

2) You have been asking yourself (or the universe) a particular question and within a short time (or instantly), the person you follow or listen to presents an answer to that very question.

3) You are studying a particular theme or creating something and in a very short time, three or more people show you the same teaching tool (person, book, podcast, photograph or so on) that relates to your theme or creation.

4) You are developing a project and the very people you need miraculously turn up in your life. This type of synchronicity can be utilised for discernment regarding the teacher you are listening to/reading, although this can occur in your life when you are not necessarily utilising discernment for anything in particular. This occurs due to the project itself being in alignment with the greater reality.

The other way synchronicity can show itself is through shape and number. Sacred geometry or numerology. This can be utilised for discernment regarding the teacher or leader you are analysing, following or listening to.

For example, they may have just written a book with a certain amount of pages in it that means something to you. You may look at the clock or at your email and see 'master numbers' such as 11.11 or 12.12. Other magickal numbers are 144 and 108.

If you are seeing double numbers like 44 or 88 or 99, this is in alignment with your bilocational consciousness and the fact that your DNA has activated beyond the third-dimensional double helix. You would be activating the second 33 and one third unit within your trinity.

If you are seeing triple numbers like 111 or 999 or 444, this is in alignment with your trilocational consciousness and the fact that your DNA has activated beyond the third-dimensional double helix. You would be activating the third 33 and one third unit within your trinity.

When these occur in alignment with the teachers and leaders you are watching, discerning, or following, then you would be an individual standing in receptivity yourself. You would be able to receive the energetic monadic light packages we spoke of earlier, that which goes beyond simple information gathering.

If you are seeing these triple numbers regularly and you know that you stand within the utilisation of the four methods we spoke of - objectivity, non-judgement, compassion and gratitude - then you yourself are absolutely ready to teach, and to teach within mastery.

Many individuals reach this stage but choose not to teach in a public sense, and prefer to remain private within their spiritual growth and knowings. They stand as the wise man or the wise woman, coming forth as the master at the exact time they are needed, on an individual level rather than a global one. These individuals are no less teachers, leaders and masters than the individual reaching thousands or millions of people.

In fact, we may quite accurately say, that there are a great many of these 'silent masters' that are activated beyond the level of many of the public and well known teachers. As we have said, *every* starseed is capable of teaching in some capacity and it is their free will and choice if and how they implement that teaching in their life.

We could say so much more regarding discernment of others when it comes to walking the path of spiritual truth seeker or cosmic explorer. The fullness of this information is beyond the scope of this transmission.

We wish to bring to you information regarding why there is disharmony and infighting amongst the truth and spiritual communities, how you can empower yourself despite the resulting confusion and chaos around you, and how to discern truth amongst the leaders and teachers who deliver their perspectives to you.

6: Alchemical Unification

You have said that the antidote to the black box programme is through 'alchemical unification'. Can you explain this?

The alchemical unification is that which we used as explanation through our model of activating all three 33 and one third aspects of self.

This, as we have said, is an extremely basic and simplified model of unification.

Yet it fits accurately with that which you are as an organic human template presentation.

We use the Holy Trinity or divine trine looking at your energetic field as units of three, as the 'quantum vesica piscis formation' if you will.

We use the Celtic triquetra as this symbolises more accurately this presentation.

The units of three are the male, female and child; or the gold, silver and rose gold - is this correct?

There are many, many ways to explain the three aspects of the energetic field. This is not just the field of the human being but also all individualised structures such as planetary systems, universes, galaxies, suns and creation itself.

So male, female and the creation between them as 'the child' on a cosmic level would translate to:

Male = the first expression or pulse.

Female = the equal and opposite reaction to that first expression or pulse (the first distortion from pure unity).

Child = 'step down Logos creations' from the first and second expressions or pulses.

This is presented in a linear sense, yet in the truest reality all occur simultaneously in one moment as wave pattern or unified field.

In a linear sense, one would place 'female' first as she is the energetic that births and creates. Yet the male energetic is the giver of that which she receives in order to birth/create, so ultimately these are intertwined in one simultaneous pulse. The child is also intertwined, as the creation and the creator are one. The Holy Trinity or divine trine depicts the unified and infinite nature of the three within the triquetra symbol.

The energetic expression of 'all that is' mirrors the expression or pulse that is creation itself. You *are* that expression or pulse. You are a holographic representation or replica, for the original pattern replicates itself over and over.

When you bring this expression into the human template, then there are infinite ways to describe the template. The reason for this is that you are describing 'an infinity'. *That is what you are.* You are an infinite structure.

To say 'male, female and child' brings the entire expression or pulse into the third-dimensional experience, so you may see what you are and how that expression or pulse is presented as all that is you.

In religions within your world, the father-mother-child has been expressed also as 'Father-Son-Holy Ghost' and 'Maiden-Mother-Crone' (as a divine feminine expression). Always a group of three, a Holy Trinity or divine trine. The 'One', the polarity expression to the 'One' and the creation.

When we present the geometry of this simplified presentation, we look at the accurate components of 33 and one third, in three units. For this is how you are made (in a geometric sense).

The balance is the three units of 33 that equal 99 - for you are this.

This equation explains the holographic and quantum nature of creation.

The 'one third' makes the original pattern recreate itself. The 'one third' is the 'stargate aspect' if you will. This is the part that allows the 33 to travel through itself into new territory, new creation. This is known as the 'MerKaVah' or 'MerKaBah'. As we have said, this is beyond the scope of this transmission. However, we provide keycodes and energetic triggers within each transmission that we deliver. Our radiation of energy towards those who receive our words is not just about the words or the message. It is a receiving of energetic frequency which contain memory activation codes or patterns within. True communication is energetic. You would know this perhaps as a combination of clairsentience, empathy and telepathy.

45

The keycodes and triggers we speak of lie in the geometric presentation of the 33 and one third Holy Trinity as the alchemical code. We could also refer to this as an 'energetic quantum template'.

Keycodes and triggers work well for all through sacred geometric presentation. Yet also the colour rays and flames hold the same patterning and coding. We speak here of 'photonic light transference'.

When we express this 'Holy Trinity' template as 'gold, silver and rose gold', the visual received by you when you utilise the visualisations goes directly to the DNA. The visualisation of gold, silver into rose gold is a code for alchemy itself.

You are communicating with/talking to the DNA when you visualise gold, silver into rose gold. You are saying, "Please activate and transform from the carbon molecule into the crystalline matrix."

You are showing the DNA how to transform. Or, more accurately, we could also say you are *making conscious* that which is naturally occurring.

The unification is there with the entire cosmic ascension process when you do this. You have particles from the galactic core, or 'photonic light codes' should we say, coming in from your Central Sun and your actual sun (Sol) and 'beaming down' onto every part of your planetary grid system.

The crystal core of your Earth changes her geometric structure in response to these particles or light codes.

Yet this same process occurs within your DNA as it is not confined to the time and space of the third dimension. DNA is matter, antimatter and the merge of these, so exists as a unified field (with information or memory codes for that unified field).

Whilst ultimately the presentation is a 144 unity structure and a 9 structure, unified zero point field (this is 'us' at this point, the White Winged Collective Consciousness of Nine), it also holds that configuration as twelve templates of twelve units.

We have presented this 144/9 unity structure as a trinity or trine, and we utilise here this simplified model for explanation that is three aspects of 33 and one third for each unit.

The DNA is receptive to this trinity presentation for it is the *same presentation* in a different format. Or rather, it is a different format to you. The 33 code, the 144 code and the 9 code are ultimately the same.

What you look at here is, let us say, the 'mother' and the 'daughter' if you will (a replication). In physical incarnation, we could express this as the 'same soul incarnating as mother and daughter'. This would be a 'quantum overlap incarnation', as in one soul incarnating in the same physical timespace reality as two individual incarnations. In geometric/mathematical terms, this is simply the same expression in another format.

You will each be called by the 144 and the 33 as *Master Numbers.*

In your reality at this current time, the trinity is showing itself to you over and over. For the structure, in its most simplified form, is a trinity as we have explained. Original pulse or expression, equal and opposite reaction and Logos creation.

So when this is created by you as gold, silver into rose gold, and you utilise the visualisation of the flame (for pre-matter looks clairvoyantly like fire), then you join with the DNA in its transformation and transmutation process.

You also join with the light codes that 'ride the wave' that moves into your dimensional space, translated as particles or light codes coming in from the galactic core, Central Sun and cosmic sun onto your planet Earth. You are intrinsically connected to the grid system of your planet and the galactic grid system.

As you transform your DNA structure from carbon to crystalline, so too do you, collectively, as the Divine Princess Aurora consciousness, transform the planetary and galactic grid systems. You link with these grid structures.

In order to 'pass through' that barrier we spoke of, in its greater presentation, it is a stargate system or system of travel or transportation (MerKaBah). Your DNA reconstruction 'matches' the galactic and planetary grid structures. It is like your DNA is the key and the planetary and galactic grid structures are the locks. You need the correct key in order to 'open the lock' if you will, or 'unlock the code'. For keycode/memory triggering, we present the word 'Key' as 'Quay'. The symbol that is 'Q' being more quantum in expression and higher in frequency than the letter in your alphabet that is 'K'. The symbol 'Q' is a code in itself but that is beyond the scope of this transmission.

Your DNA is (or contains) a code or series of codes. The planetary grid system is reached, through humanity's collective emotional 'signal' through that which you know as the Schumann resonance.

We use the description of 'Schumann resonance' due to your familiarity with that term yet this is more than just a pulse, beat or signal. The term 'Krystal river' holds genetic keycodes for you. Your memories are triggered through the phrase 'Krystal river'.

Literally, when you visualise a river flowing with crystal liquid, you communicate with the DNA in a profound and direct way. That visual of the Krystal river explains far more to you intrinsically as to what this 'resonance' actually is. This is the 'frequency signature' or 'musical note' for Earth into Gaia. It is the 'voice of Terra'.

'Krystal river' is more explanatory and more of a trigger into unity connection with the river itself, rather than the term 'Schumann resonance' which is a description named after the individual who 'discovered' it.

Yet your Schumann resonance, Krystal river was discovered long before this by not just one individual but by tribes of individuals within the time period up to your 'known history'. The one that is called 'Tesla' did much discovery, or should we say 'rediscovery', regarding the frequency signature of the Earth.

Yet long before this, the Atlantean and Lemurian civilisations knew of the Krystal river. The Lemurians worked in a very similar way to that which we present in this transmission through the rose gold flame. In fact, we could say that the trinity field presentation of gold, silver into rose gold is 'Lemurian code' if you will.

The Atlantean peoples utilised the Krystal river in a more 'technological way' (or a more scientific way). The Lemurians accepted the Krystal river as it was, they were harmonised with it. The Atlanteans wished to study it and utilise its power. This is a very simplified example of the very complex pre-known history regarding the ancient civilisations of Lemuria and Atlantis.

The one who was called Tesla simply activated his galactic and planetary memories that linked him into those time periods. You, starseeds on Earth, this is what you are doing. You are linking through the memory field system that is your DNA matrix to not only space (galactic planetary grid systems), but time (Atlantis and Lemuria). Once again, we present simplified examples of space/time unity.

You ask us of alchemical unification and this is all we have said and more. It is the chemical bonding within your physical human body, becoming unified with all things and you being 'aware' of this process. Awareness occurs and is focused within varying degrees and it matters not which 'code' you subscribe to...

Atlantis and Lemuria memory system.

MerKaBah stargate travel.

33 and one third Holy Trinity presentation.

144,000 warriors of light.

Rainbow wave pulse into Earth's biosphere.

Schumann resonance pulse connection.

Gold, silver into rose gold flame.

All these are different presentations of the same 'code'.

The code for alchemical unification which is carbon-based molecule into silicone/silicate-based 'crystalline' molecular structure (matrix). This is that which you know as 'turning lead into gold', or *unification* (with Earth, the new Earth, all planetary systems, Central Sun, Logos, God, Source, Prime Creator, original expression or pulse, living geometric masters and so on) through that which you know as memory.

This is what we mean by 'alchemical unification'.

This is the *divine marriage.*

It is a marriage within. That which we may call the male/female alignment and it is expressed in a myriad of ways upon your planet. This is understood by many but due to the different expressions, it will depend on where you are within your process of alchemical unification (how many 33 and one third units you have activated and aligned) as to how much understanding you have regarding these different expressions of the divine marriage and how you express them yourself.

Dissonance and disharmony is thus caused within the awakening starseeds, as we explained when discussing the 'infighting' within the truth movement and spiritual communities.

The misunderstandings specific to the male/female expressions and the myriad ways these are felt within the awakening population are widespread. However, you each go through a very unique and subjective journey when you move into alchemical unification.

No one person is fully immune from receiving the keycodes/light codes/waveforms from the galactic core. There are those who have blocks to the process and are 'stuck' within the overall pattern presentation of just the one 33 and one third aspect of the trinity. Yet as they resolve traumas and allow receptivity to create flow, they too will link with the Krystal river and activate memories through alchemical unification. Everyone upon your planet is 'waking up' in one way or another.

For those that have moved into alchemical unification and have two or all three unified aspects of 33 and one third activated, you will be seeing the subjective synchronistic codes that are the external representations of the 144, the 9 and the 33.

The 144 complete energetic matrix presentation (full DNA strand crystalline matrix) and the 9 (zero point unified field) and the 33 (Holy Trinity, triquetra) are all presentations of the alchemical unification through divine marriage full realisation of self, fully activated DNA strand, crystalline matrix.

We utilise, through this transmission, the Krystal river (Schumann resonance) connection and unification through the 'creation aspect' or 'third aspect' (the child of the divine marriage). This is that which is created from the unity/duality marriage of the:

Male/Female

Expression or Pulse/Distortion

Gold flame/Silver flame

Day (sun)/Night (moon)

Conscious/Subconscious

Left hemisphere of the human brain/Right hemisphere of the human brain

Matter/Antimatter

Magnetic/Electric

All these examples are different presentations of the 'divine marriage' or 'twin flame'.

The resulting creation from these unified dualistic presentations of action, and equal and opposite reaction, is *life itself.*

Within your existence upon planet Earth/mother Gaia, the 'creation grid' is the Krystal river, life force pulse that gives you life. The 'mother's milk' if you will. She keeps you alive, she nurtures you, she protects you.

This we speak of is the Krystal river (Schumann resonance) and we present to you the method of unification with this Krystal river, life giving mother's milk through the rose gold flame.

Within this transmission, 'the result' of alchemical unification is the rose gold flame. We present 'the result' before the actual unification (for those not yet in full unity expression and also for those who are!). The reason for this is due to the working of the law of magnetic attraction.

"As you think, so you are," or "You need to act as if that which you desire has already occurred/been received in order to create it."

This is the utilisation of the rose gold flame process. For if you take awareness of gold/silver into rose gold flame as the creation, before this has occurred within your fields, then you utilise the law of magnetic attraction and create it to happen. You manifest it.

When you take awareness of the Krystal river, you utilise mother's milk/Gaia's heartbeat/Schumann resonance in a conscious way. This creates activation of the matching DNA strands to the planetary grid system (and galactic grid system) through Schumann resonance activity and spiking. This does not occur 'all at once' but in accordance with your ability collectively to assimilate, integrate and process the 'energy spikes' or Schumann resonance raise.

Your conscious awareness of gold flame, silver flame into rose gold flame connects you to this 'rise and fall' or 'peaks and troughs' of the Schumann resonance/Krystal river in its quantum, sine wave form expression. This will always be the antidote to any false matrix or created scrambled signal when those that utilise the awareness of the rose gold flame (and what it signifies) do this all together simultaneously, en masse as a collective. This simultaneous awareness does not have to be at the exact same moment but can be spread across a time period, as in the '2012 consciousness shift' (which you are still in as this extends beyond 2012). From the higher perspective (antimatter reality), this extended linear time period *is* a simultaneous moment.

So you may now see why we say:

The antidote is the rose gold flame.

The antidote is the Krystal river (Schumann resonance) and ultimately, through alchemical unification, *the antidote is you.*

7: The Rose Gold Flame and the Shielding Process

As we have said, the silver ray is the feminine frequency within the body and the golden ray is the masculine frequency. When these merge or marry together (like two flints rubbing together), they create an internal fire (phire) that manifests as 'the rose gold ray' or 'rose gold flame' as it is activated.

We also used the analogy of three aspects to the trinity. Each aspect being one unit of 33 and one third. We could say that the silver (female) aspect is one 33 and one third unit and the golden (male) aspect is the second 33 and one third unit. The third 33 and one third unit is the 'creation' or the 'child' (the rose gold flame).

One symbol that shows this trinity field through geometry is the Celtic knot or 'triquetra'.

The twin flame presentation of the vesica piscis geometry depicts the masculine, the feminine and the creation as one aspect of the overall trinity, yet is a trinity in itself. Every aspect to each individualised, infinite structure is a holographic replica of the greater and the lesser aspect. Every structure is an 'emanation' of another structure.

The triquetra simply shows us the expanded presentation of the vesica piscis. A quantum version in holographic form.

Within many depictions of the triquetra, one brings a circle into the centre of the three vesica piscis geometries. This shows the aspects of the trinity and the unified whole. This depicts the entire 'journey' of the DNA, if you will.

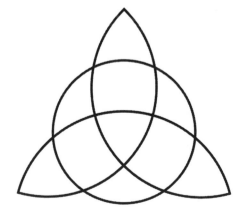

Above: The triquetra

The first exercise we show you, involving the rose gold flame and the utilisation of the Schumann resonance as the antidote to the 5G scrambled field and the black box programme, is to use the symbol of the triquetra.

There are several ways this can be done.

Firstly, you can meditate upon the triquetra simply by visualising the symbol within meditation.

You can also move into an 'open-eyed' meditation where you are in a relaxed, meditative space whilst looking at the triquetra symbol.

You can also look at the symbol as the very last image you look at before you go to sleep at night. This is especially helpful if you wish to use dream magick and dream healing as part of your antidote creation.

If you do decide to use the triquetra symbol as a trigger into dreamtime investigation/magick and healing, then you must 'prepare your sleeping space' before you do this.

If you are sleeping outdoors in nature, there is no need to prepare your space as nature has already done this for you.

Indoors, you would need to make sure all Wi-Fi and Internet signals are turned off in your home and all electronic equipment is removed from your bedroom. Make sure there is no metal within the mattress or bed frame you sleep upon, and do your best to utilise chemical-free bedding.

Having crystals in your bedroom is especially helpful. Orgonite also.

What about metal jewellery? For example, a wedding ring or a meaningful, sentimental necklace? Should these not be worn?

It is better to remove any metal jewellery from your person before sleeping, especially if you wish to move into magickal dreamtime work and healing. Metal blocks and interferes with the signal as well as supercharging the EMF and 5G fields. If this is a wedding ring that you never take off, and if it will cause you emotional distress to take it off, then it is counterproductive to your dreamtime work to remove it.

If you have wooden jewellery or crystal jewellery, these can be left on as they will enhance your dreamtime experience. Crystals especially provide a positive charge (as in a helpful energetic boost to the shielding work).

53

When it comes to wearing jewellery during your daytime waking state, then this can be most helpful. If you can find jewellery that is Celtic in design, or that holds a triple spiral pattern or triquetra and similar depictions, then these are sacred symbols themselves. These can work for you when they are in alignment with your paradigms and belief systems and intentions. This is known as 'symbol magick' or 'sigil magick' and this type of jewellery can, in itself, act as the shield. It simply amplifies the energetic system of the body when it is in alignment with the geometries formed by your cohesive thoughts.

Tattoos upon the body can act as the same type of shielding.

What about having pets or children in your bedroom when doing this dreamtime magick?

Children and animals, when they are beloved family members, are no block whatsoever to dreamtime magick and can often enhance it. Many a mother of a newborn still awakening in the night is sent into deep astral projection and out-of-body travel, as the constant awakening to see to her child is a trigger.

Animals enhance the energy in your bedroom, but none more so than the domestic cat who exists within antimatter and matter simultaneously at all times. The purr of the cat is naturally the frequency of the golden mean, Fibonacci sequence.

Within your meditation or visualisation (closed or open-eyed looking at the triquetra image), imagine that the triquetra is a brilliant and bright silver colour. Make sure you hold that beautiful silver colour in your mind's eye. You should feel an opening of the heart when doing this.

Then imagine that the triquetra symbol is becoming a golden colour, getting brighter and brighter until all the silver colour has now been replaced with the gold.

Then visualise the gold changing colour, taking on a pink hue and eventually becoming rose gold in colour.

This is a very simple but very powerful exercise. This will trigger 'downloads' within dreamtime or meditation if you are a natural medium or channel. This exercise in itself can bring about balance and natural healing.

To strengthen and boost this exercise, you can keep rose quartz crystal by your bedside. A crystal wand or a crystal skull holds even more powerful, activating energy.

When it comes to jewellery, if you can find a pendant or piece of jewellery that depicts a silver circle with a rose gold triquetra, Celtic knot entwined with the circle, this will also boost this exercise.

What you are doing here is creating allowance and receptivity within the DNA fields to the natural 'tuning fork' of the Earth that is the Schumann resonance. This creates the shield we speak of.

You will find, that as part of the antidote to the black box programme technologies, many starseeds begin to create these talismans or activating jewellery, orgonite and crystals that make up part of this shield. They are simply tools to assist, as the actual shield is your DNA and your consciousness.

Jewellery based on spiral and coil patterns, Celtic weave and triquetra, and 'Flower of Life' orgonite pendants all are boosters to the shield.

If your emotions are invested in the jewellery, then this in itself creates a 'closed circuit shield' between your emotions and the 'protections' the jewellery gives you. For example, if a loved one has transitioned to spirit, it is now quite widespread within your western communities to place tiny amounts of your loved one's ashes into the jewellery, or to wear jewellery with the loved one's fingerprints on.

These act as shields themselves due to the deep emotions held within them. The fingerprint keeps the energy field of the loved one close to you.

Wearing ashes in jewellery needs to have a permission from the individual who has transitioned as it can 'displace' the soul of the person who has passed over. This subject in itself is a whole other transmission. Just know that permission is almost always given from the vantage point of the higher self of the loved one, if unconditional love exists between the individuals.

In the case of a child wearing its parents ashes or a twin flame partner wearing their partner's ashes, permission is undoubtedly given as the comfort that is bought to the living relative creates the 'closed loop energetic circuit' and is a shield in itself, which is why we draw attention to it.

Shields that connect into Schumann resonance fields can also be created through water.

Swimming in natural ocean water is an extremely powerful shield as the Schumann resonance is amplified through the oceans upon your planet. This can be recreated within your own bathtubs at home using Himalayan salts or any magnesium-based salts. Certain aromatherapy creations and herbs can also create shielding, as can placing crystals within the bathtub.

The only case where it is not advisable to create a water shield in your bathtub, is when your bath is made of metal. This would scramble the signal and have the opposite effect (as in, lack of shield and focus away from Schumann resonance).

The most powerful material for creating a water shield is stone such as crystal, followed by wood. A crystal bathtub full of sea salt is an absolute replica of the ocean and creates a 'super conductor' directly into the Schumann resonance fields.

We also recommend you utilise a heavy metal detoxification programme. The reason for this is that metals within the organic human body system can 'lock on' to the Wi-Fi 5G scrambled system and amplify it, so cleansing from heavy metals within the body is a shield in itself. The dark green leafy vegetables from the land and the seaweeds from unpolluted waters are able to chelate these heavy metals from the body. We recommend the blue-green algae also, such as chlorella and spirulina.

Utilising the Rose Gold Flame

As we have said, there are many methods of creating the shield and we have given shielding techniques such as talisman creation, dreamtime work, sigil magick through the triquetra, water shield creation and heavy metal detoxification. We now provide for you exercises with the rose gold flame.

When you visualise the rose gold flame, you create an image in your mind's eye that 'activates' through the pineal gland visual cortex system. The rose gold (and indeed the symbol of the rose itself) is a known symbol within what we may call the 'cosmic alphabet' or the 'language of light'.

When you visualise the rose gold flame, you speak directly to the DNA. When you create the rose gold flame as a shield, then the molecular structure within your body as silicate/crystalline follows suit (through a process similar to that which is known as 'cymatics') and your entire energy field naturally keys into the Schumann resonance.

If enough individuals hold this belief system and follow similar spiritual exercises, then collectively the Schumann resonance will be spiked and kept at a high enough frequency to 'drown out' the 5G network and chemical bombardment.

Either in meditation or in a relaxed state, we would ask you to visualise a silver candle and a gold candle. Both these candles burn one flame each. The silver candle burns a golden flame. The gold candle burns a silver flame.

Sit with this visualisation for a few minutes, simply watching the candles and the burning flames.

This exercise balances the right and left hemispheres of the brain, as well as communicating directly with the DNA about the shielding technique you are employing. The intrinsic intelligence within the cellular structure of the entire bodymind knows what you are doing.

After a while, we would ask you to draw the candles closer and closer together until the silver candle burning a golden flame and the gold candle burning a silver flame become one candle and one flame.

As the candles merge together, gold and silver, the colour of the candle begins to turn a beautiful rose colour with a matching rose coloured flame. Yet the sparkle of the gold remains, creating a rose gold colour.

You are now watching a rose gold candle burning a rose gold flame, and you are fully aware that the rose gold is a merge of the silver and the gold.

Know that the right hemisphere of the brain (silver) and the left hemisphere of the brain (gold) have created a unified brain pattern, where the left and right hemispheres are in equal balance.

Within the pineal gland, a beautiful diamond liquid crystal of a metallic rose gold colour has been created. This rose gold crystal liquid then seeps down from the brain stem into the throat, and you visualise yourself drinking this rose gold liquid. Know that this is 'ambrosia' or indeed 'nectar of the Gods'.

As you drink this delicious and sweet nectar, you visualise the flame of the rose gold candle getting bigger and bigger.

The rose gold flame begins to surround you, like a ring of fire around you. The candle has unified with the flame and now, sitting in sacred space, there is just you surrounded by the rose gold flame ring of fire.

Allow this ring of fire to completely surround you until it eventually becomes a ball of fire, like a rose-gold-pink orb, with you sitting in the centre, nurtured and protected.

This is the love of the divine mother. This is the protective and nurturing space of the cosmic womb.

Physiologically, what you are doing is connecting your frequencies to the like frequencies of the planetary mother - the Gaia-Earth mother - and her protective and life-giving heartbeat, the Schumann resonance.

You are more powerful than you can possibly know. We have gone some way to explain to you within this transmission of the power you have, especially when you join with like vibrational 'other'.

The starseeds are like vibrational 'other'. Yet when you sit in sacred meditation, taking the mantra that is 'OM' or 'AUM', you make the sound that is 'M'.

Add this primordial mantra to 'other' (your other alternative selves) and you create the word 'mother'. What you do here is take the preform or antimatter and create matter (mother). The matter/mother is the mother Gaia-Earth and the Schumann resonance is her heartbeat.

Connecting electrically and magnetically to the Schumann resonance through the 'language of light' frequency colour of the rose gold flame is just one method to key your fields into the loving, nurturing embrace of the 'Earth-Gaia shield' that is the Schumann resonance.

It is possible for those fully centred within the trinity (all three 33 and one third aspects activated) to utilise cosmic shields as well as the Earth-Gaia shield. You can utilise the Pleiadian shield, the Sirian shield, the Lyran shield or the Arcturian shield. These techniques are beyond the scope of this transmission, except to say that the 'Schumann resonances' upon all these planetary bodies are rising in frequency just like that of Earth.

For the majority of starseeds, connecting to the Earth-Gaia shield is all you will need to do in order to create the protective barrier from chemicals and from scrambled electrical microwave fields like 5G.

So, in summary of this transmission:

1) There is an antidote to all things. Polarity must be kept in balance. The collective consciousness of the starseeds is the antidote.

2) The Schumann resonance can be utilised as an antidote to black box programme technologies. The Schumann resonance, known also as the Krystal river, flows through you and is part of you.

3) There is disharmony within the leaders of the truth community and the spiritual teachers. There is also much truth and activation to be found here. All starseeds are potential teachers, leaders and healers.

4) Discernment is found through objectivity, non-judgement, compassion and gratitude. Synchronicity is a clue to your own activation and to being on track with your spiritual development and awareness.

5) The merging of the silver (feminine) and the golden (masculine) creates the rose gold (child/creation). The rose gold flame can be utilised to connect to the antidote, that of the Schumann resonance, and create a shield from black box programme technologies and similar inverted matrix fields.

As ever, we wish you most well on your journey of evolution, awakening, enlightenment and ascension. We observe you and, within that objective omnipresent space of observation, we hold for you the very brightest of rose gold flames. We hand to you these rose gold flames for you are, indeed, the torchbearers of Gaia. We bow to you in service, in gratitude and always with complete, humble and unconditional love.

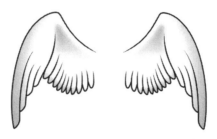

We are the

White Winged Collective Consciousness of Nine

Enjoy this book?

Check out magentapixie.com

* Vast Video Archive of Magenta Pixie's Messages *

* Guided Meditations * Interviews * Lectures * Free Stuff *

Other books by Magenta Pixie, available in print and Kindle editions

~ Masters of the Matrix ~

~ Divine Architecture and the Starseed Template ~

~ The Infinite Helix and the Emerald Flame ~

"Look no further, all is explained in this book, encapsulating all religious texts and then explaining further. All answers are given and accessible by all, it only takes an open heart of unconditional love and you too can have all the secrets of all realities revealed to you."

Amazon customer review for *The Infinite Helix and the Emerald Flame*

Made in the USA
San Bernardino, CA
19 March 2020

66044989R00035